100 First Animal Words for Toddlers

100 First Animal Words for Toddlers

JAYME YANNUZZI

Illustrations by **Sarah Rebar**

**ROCKRIDGE
PRESS**

To my daughter, my greatest accomplishment and favorite student. Reading with you in my lap is my favorite place to be. I love you. —JY

First Rockridge Press hardcover edition 2022

Originally published in trade paperback by Rockridge Press 2022

Rockridge Press and the Rockridge Press logo are trademarks or registered trademarks of Callisto Media Inc. and/or its affiliates in the United States and other countries and may not be used without written permission.

For general information on our other products and services or to obtain technical support, please contact our Customer Care Department within the United States at (866) 744-2665, or outside the United States at (510) 253-0500.

Hardcover ISBN: 979-8-88608-488-7
Paperback ISBN: 978-1-63878-387-9
eBook ISBN: 978-1-63878-554-5

Manufactured in the United States of America

Series Designer: Amanda Kirk
Interior and Cover Designer: Richard Tapp
Art Producer: Alyssa Williams
Editor: Jeanann Pannasch
Production Editor: Nora Milman
Production Manager: Holly Haydash

Illustrations © 2022 Sarah Rebar
Illustrator photo courtesy of Jeff Fried

10 9 8 7 6 5 4 3 2 1 0

Dear Reader,

I am so excited for you to use this book with your toddler! For our little readers, animals—and the sounds they make—are some of the most memorable first words. This book will introduce your toddler to exciting new animals and words to add to their growing vocabulary.

Here are a few tips for using this book:

- Point to the pictures on each page, say the animal words, and use them in sentences.

- Ask questions about what your child notices on each page. You can ask, "What animal are you pointing to?" or "What sound does this animal make?"

- Play a game of "I Spy": "I spy with my little eye . . . an animal that says, 'Moo!' Yes, a cow!"

- Gather animal toys or figurines from your home and place them in a bag. Select one and have your toddler match the figurine to the animal in the book.

Use this book to read, talk, and play with your toddler over and over again.

alligator

alpaca

anteater

antelope

armadillo

baboon

bat

bear

beaver

bee

camel

cat

cow

crab

deer

dog

dolphin

duck

eagle

eel

elephant

emu

firefly

fish

flamingo

fox

frog

giraffe

goat

goose

gorilla

grasshopper

hamster

hawk

hippopotamus

horse

ibis

iguana

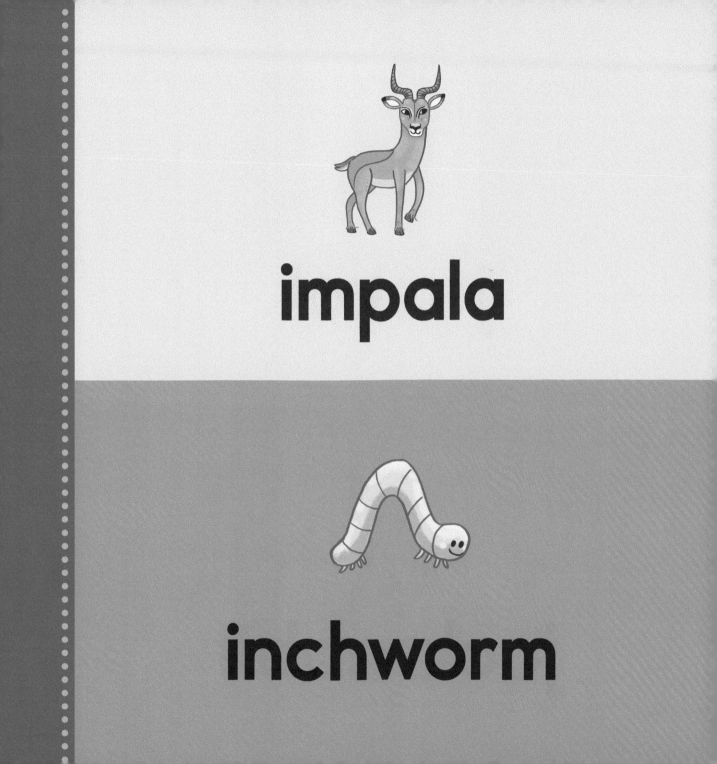

impala

inchworm

jackal

jackrabbit

jaguar

jellyfish

kangaroo

kiwi

koala

Komodo dragon

ladybug

lamb

lion

llama

lobster

manatee

manta ray

moose

mouse

mule

narwhal

newt

nighthawk

numbat

octopus

opossum

otter

owl

ox

panda

parrot

penguin

pig

porcupine

quail

quokka

raccoon

rat

reindeer

rhinoceros

seahorse

seal

shark

skunk

spider

tiger

toad

toucan

turkey

turtle

umbrella bird

urchin

viper

vulture

walrus

whale

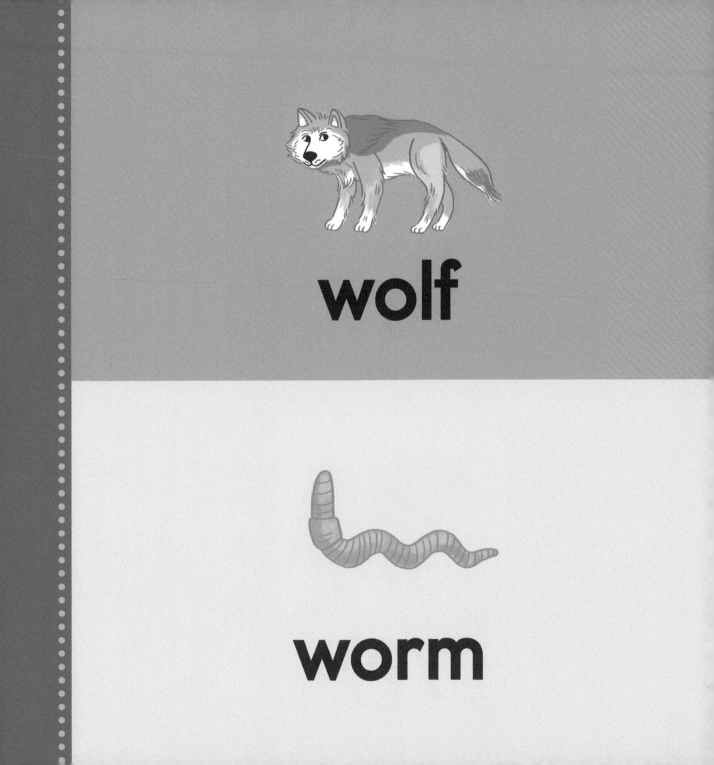

wolf

worm

x-ray fish

yak